The Logistics of a Whitewashed Virgin

By

Michelle R. Taylor

Edited by: Bevette Thomas

The Logistics of a Whitewashed Virgin

Text Copyright© 2014 by Michelle R. Taylor

Published by C.D. Extravaganza Publishing
6111 Winsome Lane #88
Houston, TX 77057
www.CDExtravaganza.com

This book is a biography. Some names, characters, businesses, organizations, places events and incidents are the product of the author's imagination or are used fictionally. Any resemblance of actual persons, living or dead, events or locales is entirely coincidental.

No part of this book may be reproduced in any form or by any electronic or mechanical means including information storage and retrieval systems, without permission in writing from the author. The only exception is by a reviewer, who may quote short excerpts in a review.

Taylor, Michelle R., 2014
The Logistics of a Whitewashed Virgin: a book by Michelle R. Taylor. -1rst ed.
C.D. Extravaganza Publishing 2014

Summary: The Logistics of a Whitewashed Virgin is a revealing biography about a young girl's journey through school and how she dealt with common social and academic issues that most young people go through. It is a survival guide to inspire all young ladies to conquer challenges and pursue all of their endeavors.

ISBN: 978-0-692-22255-3
{Girls – Guide – High School – College – Self-Esteem – Motivational}

Genre: Teen Biography/Non-Fiction/How-To
Cover Design: M. Taylor

Printed in the United States of America

CONTENTS

Forward Me…………………………………..Page 1

Chapter 1- Background Me……………..Page 4

Chapter 2 – Whitewashed Me…………..Page 13

Chapter 3 – Elementary Me……………..Page 23

Chapter 4 – Girl Scout Me……………….Page 35

Chapter 5 – Middle Me……………………Page 45

Chapter 6 – High School Me…………….Page 62

Chapter 7 - College Me……………………Page 81

Chapter 8 – Future Me……………………Page 117

Forward Me:

Finally! It is time for me to graduate. It has definitely been a long time coming. People are amazed that I am graduating from college so early. Yep, it only took me three years. One reason for my fast pass through academia is taking dual credits in high school. I recommend taking dual credits in high school. It makes college life so much easier. The other reason for my fast pass is no sex, my party ethics and never feeling the need to be in a big group. Yes, I said NO SEX. I know it's hard for most people to believe that a college student my age has never had sex. Well, it's true. I have no shame, and I claim my fame by focusing on my studies, doing what I needed to do, while always being me.

Many people have made up in their minds why girls like me do so well in school. People think girls like me are nerds, non-sociable, uppity, and weird. The worst thing that people assume is that if you don't have a boyfriend and have not had sex, you must be a lesbian. Unfortunately, it is typical for society to put labels on people because of common stereotypes. If you don't act like everyone else, then something is wrong with you. Well, I never liked acting like someone other than who I am. Peer pressure has never been a problem for me.

I hope this book will encourage all those girls who enjoy being what I call quirky-cool, and don't mind defying the labels of a pre-determined social normality. Shake off the pressures of family, peers and society. If you want less pressure, be you! I say those people who try to be so "normal" are wannabes. I choose the unique quirky-cool me any day. The rest are LAME!

Chapter 1- Background Me:

How did I become so quirky and cool? I guess you can say, I was grown this way. Our parents, plant the seeds and then they put us in a special pot with *their* fertilizer, but eventually, we grow out of that pot and the rest of the world shapes us. All we can do is hope for enough water. Who knows how far we will grow, where we will grow or how long we will grow. I just know for a fact that we grow. Some of us are weeds. Some of us are bushes and some of us are tall trees. I like to think of myself as an ivy growing in different ways, but never stopping, and although there may be guidelines, I continue on my path with abundant growth.

We all start our growth by watching and learning from the main people in our lives and usually that is our parents. Although we want to think we are nothing like our parents, we are! We actually pick up what is called idiosyncrasies from the people we are around most of the time. It is one reason some of us argue and defy our parents during those wonderful teen years. We are becoming them. I know it sounds like a scary movie, but it is not so bad later on in life. I do mean extremely later in life. I know I picked up a few of my mom's behaviors, although she says I am like my father. She only says that when she is angry with me or I do something she feels is ridiculous. Get ready girls, you are probably more like your mom than you know and the same with the boys and their dads.

The good behaviors I have picked up from my mom include independence, perception and assertiveness. My father probably would say I forgot, "bossiness." True! However, sometimes girls must be the boss and lay down our law. Girls of today must stand their ground and let no guy walk all over them. He may be cute, but no boy is so cute that he should be allowed to mentally or physically abuse you. I have seen too many of my friends change who they are and who they wanted to become because of some guy. I say, "If he can't deal with your quirky-cool ways, then he is not worth the ground you walk on!" Don't settle for the lame. Remember, you are growing in many directions, so he can follow, catch up or get left behind. There is someone out there that matches your dreams and aspirations. I say wait! Make good friends and have your kind of fun. YOLO! It is better than getting with someone who you might hate later. Save yourself and the taxpayer's money from going through a lengthy divorce, child support, stepparents, arguments and.... too much? I know, but it happens.

The Logistics of a Whitewashed Virgin

I embraced my strengths early on, including the bossiness. The way I perceive bossiness is not about bossing others. It is about being in control of me and being the boss of me. I decide what I do and how I want to do it. Of course, I listen to my parents and respect authority, but when it comes to choices I have to make on my own, I make sure that I will not regret them later. I make mistakes, but they are my mistakes. I can fix them. I do not blame others for my choices. Well, sometimes I blame my mother, but who doesn't? The problem with some people is that they never fix their mistakes or they take too long to do so. I will go into details about my brother, but.... if you have a little brother, you know what I am talking about. The bottom line is take responsibility and face the consequences. I say own it, solve it and move on. Don't hold things against yourself, and definitely don't let others hold your mistakes against you. If they cannot move on, then move on without them.

Being the boss of me has deflected peer pressure. If I feel that I am being pressured, I will do the complete opposite of what my peers expect. I remember playing on the playground at recess in elementary and there was this one girl that nobody wanted to play with. I don't know why and I did not care. I left the people I was playing with to play with her. I remember one of my friends asking me why I was playing with the girl. I did not answer because I thought it was a ridiculous question. I continued playing with her every day. She was very creative and we would laugh and have a good time. She made up new games. Eventually, others wanted to play the games. The girl left the school at the end of the year. The next time I saw her was on TV. I can't say who she is, but I remember she was on a talk show and she was talking about bullying. Apparently, she had been bullied most of her childhood. She told the talk show host that the bullying stopped after she met one girl that did not mind playing with her at recess. She did not mention my name, but I believe she was talking about me. It was not anything special to me. All I did was not listen to others and I found a new friend. My philosophy on dealing with peers is, we can walk the same way, but I never walk behind. If I do walk behind, it is because I am listening, learning and observing. Eventually, I will move up to the front and beyond. If I don't like what I see or feel it is not progressive to my goals, I will walk away with a big smile.

Overall, early me was about having fun the way I saw it. It was not about peer pressure or trying to fit in. It was about being me. I am genuinely me. I hate fakeness. I remember a friend once called me consistent. At first, I was worried that consistent meant boring. Later, I realized that people liked me being consistent. They can trust me and they know I will tell the truth. The same friend that called me consistent also told me some years later, "Thank you for always being there for me, even when I strayed and was not there for you."

Chapter 2 - Whitewashed Me

Whitewashed is also a term I have been labeled. According to the dictionary, the word whitewashed can mean several things. It can be the way you add white to walls and other surfaces or it can be a derogatory term used to describe minorities who have assimilated into American society. I don't see it as a derogatory term. I see it as okay! It happens! It especially happens depending on how you grew up, the people you hang around and what schools you attended. It only becomes a derogatory term when people use it to make a person feel as if they have let their heritage go to become white. I think that is ridiculous because I can only be who I am. I cannot turn white. I can have different experiences that broaden my social and academic skills, but I cannot change my race and I do not want to change my race. "I'm black and I'm proud," as they use to say back in the days.

I remember one of my cousins saying, I talk white. I was eleven and I did not know what he meant by it. "You sound like white people." I had been in predominately white schools most of my life and to me everyone spoke the same. The only thing I could think of was, I did not "talk ghetto." I did not actually have a meaning for ghetto at eleven. I knew what I heard people say on television and in my family about speaking ghetto. To me, it meant speaking broken language and using a lot of slang words, and since we were from the south it also meant adding a few southern words like "yall" or "aint" to the language. Therefore, when my cousin said I sounded white, I asked him what he meant. "You know talking all proper and stuff," he said. Proper! You mean speaking correctly, so people can understand what I am saying? What is wrong with using proper English? I asked with an attitude because I thought he was being ridiculous. "You probably think you are white," he said in a sarcastic tone. I replied. "No! I think I can read and do work at my grade level unlike you who are two grades behind and read on a third grade level." Yes, I was angry. My cousin got mad and we began arguing until my mom came in the room. "She called me ghetto!" my cousin said. "Well he called me white!" I said. My mother had a funny look on her face. I know it sounded crazy. My cousin and I laugh at it now, but it was a big deal then.

My mother explained two things to us that day, dialect and vocabulary. She said dialect is a form of language spoken in certain areas or by a certain social class. It is usually characterized by the use of certain vocabulary, grammar and pronunciation. "It is like saying y'all. Most people do not use the word y'all in northern states. It is mostly a southern dialect." My mom also told us that the use of vocabulary is very important in determining dialect, but also in determining how much a person knows. "So being ghetto is dumb," I said with a snooty, mean attitude while looking at my cousin. Of course we started arguing again, until my mom got between us and stopped it. My mom explained that using terms to degrade someone like saying, "You talk ghetto or you talk white," is street slang. She also said that "People speak differently for many reasons. The important thing to remember is to continue your education and learn everything you can. Reading is so important in learning how to talk, understand and communicate. Your dialect does not matter as long as people understand what you are saying and you are able to use words that compliment your age and development." My mom is a teacher, so sometimes her conversations sound like teaching moments, but she is right. I think my cousin learned more that day than I did because he is now an English professor.

My mom was right because I now know people with different dialects that speak very well and they are not white. The way a person speaks has nothing to do with being white. It has to do with what you learned, how you learned it and how you apply it. I don't hear people saying, "You are talking white" much anymore. I do have a friend who moved and changed schools when we were in high school to a predominately black high school. I remember her telling me that some of the students were calling her "white girl" because of how she spoke. It did not cause her any problems. She said, "Maybe I will get everyone to talking like me and there will be no differences. We will just be talking." Now that is what I call having a great quirky-cool attitude.

To me being whitewashed is a good thing because it means you have experienced diversity. You know perspectives from different races and cultures. It is important for me to go out in the world and be able to work and get along with all types of people. I do not have to agree with everything everybody believes in, but I can show understanding and keep an open mind. I enjoy being me and I love my heritage, but I love knowing other people from different backgrounds. I would not trade my education or friends I have met for anything in this world. It has made me who I am today and I treasure it. I feel sorry for people who only know one set of people and one set of rules. Sounds boring, and you cannot be quirky-cool if you are boring.

I define myself as knowing that I am part of a progression of great ancestors claiming my opportunities and victories. I never want to be stuck in any stereotypical expectation of how to act and what choices to make. I have never had any problems with racism that I have noticed because my confidence blocks all that negativity. Plus, I do not surround myself with narrow minded people. I have heard stories from my mother's experiences while attending the same schools I did, but my generation is not caught up in bashing people because of the color of their skin. However, I do know that there are people who are stuck in the past and cannot see pass skin color. I say, GET OVER IT! The world has changed and we are moving forward not backwards. I enjoy being able to learn different languages and eat foods from different countries. I encourage talking to all types of people from different places. Open up your world and see the beauty in front of you. If there are people around you that are ignorant to the opportunities of diversity, try to invite them into a new world. If they cannot handle it, move on! The world is a big place. Be the boss and explore it. I am!

Chapter 3-Elementary Me

The types of schools I attended early on were a big part of why I am who I am. My elementary school was a great foundation and my middle school got me through that identity phase. High school was more about the academic me. I am grateful to all my teachers and friends in elementary and middle school that provided a sound foundation for my future endeavors. I loved my elementary school. Parker Elementary was more than a simple elementary school. It was diverse, rigorous and filled with the magic of music. It was the perfect school for developing my quirky-coolness.

The Logistics of a Whitewashed Virgin

Academically, Parker was rigorous and diverse in its teachings. The teachers made sure all of the students were exposed to the classics in education as well as new innovations. Because of what I learned at Parker, I became interested in different cultures and different points of view. Being able to understand other cultures and points of view opened my mind to celebrating differences and knowing that there is more out there in the world than what I see in my immediate area. This led me to seek out other cultures through reading, music and friendships. I believe it is important not to live in a box of only what surrounds you. If you never venture out to see what others are doing and what is going on beyond your comfort zone, you will miss out on opportunities and become complacent and boring. If you are a person who has problems with friendships or the people around you don't except your quirky coolness, look outside your comfort zone. Trust me, your new friends are out there and they are just as quirky and cool. It is okay to be a loner, but don't let it take over your growth and progress. Join clubs and organizations that relate to the things you like. If your school does not have anything, look out in the community. Sometimes us quirky people can be best friends with our computers, but we must remember to be a part of the people world. The computer will be there when you get back.

My generation knows that our social interactions start on the playground in elementary. It can make you or break you. Parents, if you want to know what is going on in your children's elementary school life, I suggest, you ask specifically what happened on the playground. The playground and recess is an elementary kid's social outlet. It is the first club, organization, singles meet up and business meeting spot. It is amazing that on the playground kids converse about school politics, relationships, and yes, SEX! I know parents think elementary students are too young for those types of categories, but it is where it all begins. There are always kids who know more than others about life because they see it on TV or they see it live in their own families. Of course, being that elementary kids are young and immature, the conversations are usually abundantly immature and misinformed.

On the playground, I was the girl who was everybody's friend. I did not have a BFF or a particular clique. Mostly, I played with whoever was in my class. I think in kindergarten through second grade, everybody mostly played with each other. As we got older, I became the consistent listener. There is that word consistent again. In fourth and fifth grades, kids loved to tell me all the gossip. The gossip at that age among the girls was mostly about boys and who liked who. The boys mainly talked about....nothing important. It is true that we mature faster than they do, especially mentally. Sorry boys, but we start thinking about how we look, who is looking at us and what we will look like tomorrow in elementary. Whereas, boys are thinking about..NOTHING!

The sex games on the playground come in when kids play certain games that involve hiding, finding, touching and kissing. Yes parents, all of this in thirty minutes on a playground! I never played these games because I was not interested in boyfriends. I did notice some boys were good looking, but I did not have those type of feelings. However, many girls I knew on the playground were at the beginning of "I need a man," "He is my man," and "Don't look at my man." The problem is they were only boys and once again they only thought about..NOTHING! As the consistent listener, I heard all types of stories about what went on at the playground and at birthday parties. All I will say to parents and future parents is keep all doors open and always check every room. Age means nothing when hormones start to creep up. There are a lot of breakups in elementary. Breakups equal drama. Drama can lead into the classroom. I remember in fourth grade, a friend of mine could not finish her test because of a breakup. The teacher thought she had test anxiety, we all knew she had boyfriend anxiety.

Elementary drama helped me to realize how ridiculous relationships can be. I thought a lot of the drama ridden girls were silly. I thought they were wasting time on things that could wait until we got older. I enjoyed being a kid. I enjoyed not having all of those mixed up feelings and problems that was vented to me daily on the playground. It helped me to know that boyfriends could wait until I was ready to handle it. I also hate to look ridiculous and I thought all that drama was ridiculous. It was not for me. There was plenty of time for boyfriends. Maybe in middle school, I would become one of those boyfriend hunting drama mamas. Yeah, right!

Elementary is also where I noticed that being black was different than being white to some people. I did not have the problems you hear about that people had back in the old days. However, I remember when a little white girl in kindergarten asked me why my hair looked funny. I did not think it looked funny. I wore ponytails with colorful barrettes like most little black girls. I thought that was normal. Although, there was the one time that my mom combed my hair into two big afro puffs. I looked like Mickey Mouse. I was so upset. I wanted her to take it down, but my mom thought I looked cute. After a few fits and a nine year old's tantrum, I still did not get my way. My mom did not care and took me to school. I remember running into the school and straight into the restroom. I found a brush in my backpack that I left there after a sleepover. I recombed my hair and made two ponytails on each side of my head. After school my mother said, "Oh you want to be a big girl and do your own hair? Well do it by yourself tomorrow." I think she thought it would look messy, and I would learn my lesson. Actually, I was happy to do my own hair and it looked good. From then on, I've done my hair by myself. I think my mother was a little jealous because it looked better than she thought

The little girl continued to tease me about my hair daily. I told my mother and she said, "God gave everyone their beauty. Tell the little girl that your hair is beautiful, natural and full of heritage." She also told me, "If the little girl needs to know more about black hair, tell her you will be happy to teach her and give her more information." My mother is always making everything about education. The little girl did say something about my hair and I told her what my mother said. Thankfully, she never bothered me again.

Elementary definitely starts to shape who we become, but it is not the end. Everything starts to change and the realization of who you are and who the people are around you start to become prevalent in a big way in middle school.

Chapter 4-Girl Scout Me

Girl Scouts was such an important part of my development that I must dedicate an entire chapter on its positive aspects. Most girls join girl scouts in elementary and are finished during elementary. Not me! I was a girl scout from kindergarten through ninth grade. After ninth grade, I was in Girl Scout clubs like Girl Scout choir and event planning through the senior council. In eleventh and twelfth grade, I worked at the Girl Scout shop. So you see Girl Scouts is a big part of who I am.

At first, Girl Scouts was about hanging out with my friends. My mom was the leader of our troop and most of my friends in our troop were from my neighborhood. The rest of the girls were from my school. It was a very diverse troop at first. Half of the members were black girls from my neighborhood and the other half were white girls from my school. There were also Hispanics and Asians mixed into the group. We had a lot of fun going to workshops, camp and doing all kind of fun activities. I recommend putting girls into Girl Scouts. You learn about responsibility, friendships, work ethics, diversity, creativity, other cultures, etc. Everything I love today.

Girl Scouts had mostly good experiences, but there were a few experiences that would also shape my outlook on life. The first was at camp. I started going to camp in the summers during fourth grade. It was so much fun. Sometimes, I went to weekend camps. Every camp was different, but the one I liked the most was the camp with horseback riding. By time I got to sixth grade, camp was not much fun because of the changing attitudes of some of the girls. Just like in school, you had different cliques at camp. Mostly everyone got along, but there was always a set of "mean girls." They would talk about anyone that they considered weak. Usually, we stayed in a cabin that held about twelve girls. One time, the mean girls had talked so much about another girl that she did not want to do any of the daily activities. One day I went to the room to change my shirt and she was crying on her bed. I knew what was wrong. I told her to come with me to the next activity. If nobody was going to be her friend, I definitely was going to be her friend. She was surprised that I asked, but happy to come along. We went out to do an arts and craft project. When we sat down, we began talking and laughing along with a few other girls. The mean girls looked my way, but they did not say anything to me. They knew better. I don't say that as if I am the big bad wolf, but the way you carry yourself can go a long way. I always carry myself as a friendly person who is very confident about me. I don't seem needy and I don't try to impress people so they can be my friends. Those "mean girl" vultures only prey on the weak. The girl continued to hang with me and the others and had no more problems. I don't know if those mean girls ever talked to her and I did not care. When you have that type of behavior, you become insignificant to me. "Poof be gone vultures!", I say. However, it did make camp less attractive to me. I did not go to camp for drama and mess. After my seventh grade year, I stopped going to summer camp. I did participate in a few weekend camps, but that soon got old as well.

The other Girl Scout moment that would enrich my outlook on life was the reason I changed troops. From kindergarten through sixth grade I was in my mother's troop and it was fun. We did so many great things, and like I said earlier, most of the troop were friends from my neighborhood. Eventually, it was only people from my neighborhood and one girl from my school. My troop became an all-black troop with one Filipino girl. I had known all of them since kindergarten. The rest of the white girls left for different reasons and no more joined after fifth grade. Once again the attitudes of the girls started to change. They began forming little cliques among our troop. One day we went on a day trip to a local university that was holding a girls engineering day. They were showing girls about the profession of engineering. I notice some of the girls walking slow and whispering to each other. When we got on the University shuttle to go to our car, I looked back at about three of them whispering and I said to another girl, "They need to be quiet." They heard me and one of them said, "Shut up fat girl." The rest of them laughed. I was not fat, but I was a little bit bigger than those three. My mother heard them and told them that was not what sisterhood and the Girl Scouts were about. She had become tired of their attitudes.

Next, I heard them call her fat. Lucky for them, she did not hear them, but I did tell her later. She decided to talk to the parents of the three girls. Two of the girls were sisters and when she told their mom, she smiled and said she would talk to them. When my mom told the other girl's mom, she laughed in my mom's face and said, "You know how girls can be." My mom was very upset. She does not like bullies and especially when you are supposed to be on the same team. My mom was fed up, and told me that this would be the last year for our troop. She knew I wanted to join another troop with my friends from school. The parents were no help, so she ended the troop at the end of my sixth grade year. My mom explained to me that she will never put me in a situation where I am uncomfortable. "I cannot change the world or fight all of your battles, but when I can prevent a problem, I will.", She said sadly. I hated to lose my friends, but it was time to move on. Things had changed. They had changed. We eventually moved and I lost contact with many of those girls. I do have some of them as Facebook friends, but that is all. I knew that day what makes a friend and what kind of people I wanted around me. I support my friends no matter what and I expect the same back. Sometimes it is hard to make friends, but make sure you know your true friends. Don't always look for big groups or the popular group. Sometimes that one friend is the best friend. Forget about popular. You are popular and people should want to hang with you because of you. If they don't, let them go. It is their loss. Remember, quirky cool is not for everyone. We are unique!

I went on to another troop with four other girls from my original troop. Only two of us stayed in the troop for two more years. We had fun, but once again diversity won. It was about what we were learning from Girl Scouts and not messy gossip. It set the standards for my future endeavors.

Chapter 5-Middle Me

Middle school is a big turning point in most kid's life. I did not know what to expect. I thought middle school was going to be similar to elementary because most of the kids I went to elementary with attended the same middle school. I was wrong. Middle school was a whole new beast.

I think everyone goes through an identity change or crisis in Middle school. There are no more playgrounds. The playing stops and reality seeps in. It is the place where you find your identity. You start worrying more about how you look, talk, walk, dress, breathe etc. At first, I was not worried. I knew mostly everyone, so it would be the same as elementary. I was totally wrong. I started noticing changes in people the first day of school. People had grew taller, changed their hair, started wearing makeup, and although we wore uniforms, girls were wearing things tighter and shorter. I was consistent. The word consistent would become like a curse for me as the years went by. I look back at pictures from my first year of middle school, and I ask myself why? Why did I have those jeans on? Why did I wear those shoes? If you looked up the word dork, it would have a picture of me in sixth grade middle school with those ugly jeans and that bad hairstyle. If only my mother would let me burn those pictures. I know she is waiting to bring those pictures out for something special. Oh no! My graduation! I must destroy those pictures.

My later years of middle school are when I developed a sense of who I wanted to be. I found my identity; my group. It definitely was the beginning of quirky. It all started with my love of reading. Reading opened up a whole new world. I went from watching my favorite TV shows to loosing myself into a world of books. I do believe books can take you to different places, and will lead you to a curiosity of real adventures. My adventures in reading started with the regular books that my teachers made me read. I think we had a different book every month and I could not wait until the next book. I also joined the Book of the Month Club and read those award winning books. I forgot what the name of the award was, but I remember all the books had a gold sticker on them. I loved it, but it would be manga books that helped begin my road to quirky cool.

My new manga obsession started in class one day when I saw my friend Stephanie reading a book called Rave Master. I watched an anime show called Rave Master, so I was surprised to see a book with the same title. When I asked Stephanie about the book, she informed me that many of my anime shows had books about them. I was intrigued. Stephanie loaned me a few manga books, and the rest is obsessive history. I loved manga so much back in those days that I have boxes and boxes of manga books. I think I went to the bookstore every two weeks. Manga books for sale! I say that now, but I treasured my manga books for years. I still treasure them! If I do sell them, it will only be to true manga fans.

You have to be a true fan to understand the love of manga. Most manga fans started out like I did, watching anime. If you are an anime fan from my generation, you remember when "Hokage Sense" died.

The Logistics of a Whitewashed Virgin

Oh my God! I cried so much. Everyone cried. My brother even cried. Of course, he will say he didn't. It became an obsession. After I got more into reading manga, I stopped watching television. In fact, by the time I reached the tenth grade, I did not need a TV in my room. It was all manga all the time. I think one of the most exciting manga memories was when we moved three minutes from a bookstore that carried all types of manga. I was in manga paradise.

My personality determined what type of manga I read. Manga is Japanese comic strips. There are different types; science fiction, sports, romance, mystery, and sexual. The sexual types are the ones that can be a little risky, but they tell a good story. It is comedy mixed with drama. Manga may seem like cartooned comic strips to the average reader, but we manga fans know it is cutting edge drama. It is not your average kid cartoons. You have to be a mature minded person to read manga. Manga helped to develop my outlook on my changing world. It definitely made me more open minded to culture, race, and friendships. In fact, a few of my friends and I formed a manga club that met in the school library every morning before class. I miss those days.

  Friendships have always been easy for me, but it was not about who they were. It was more about what they liked. In middle school there are always different groups. Of course you have the regular groups like those that think they are popular, athletes, over achievers, too mature for school or should I say over aged students, and many more. In a diverse school, sometimes you can even get a group of all black kids. It is not that they are prejudice against other races it is that they find common ground with likes and dislikes, actions and reactions, attractions and distractions. Although I'm black, I did not fit into that group because I liked many things that were not common to the black community, like manga. Of course, I liked all types of music and had black friends, but I did not do all the same things they liked to do. Also, my preference of music could be a little different. At that time, I was into Green Day, Good Charlotte, Evanescence, etc. However, I did like Beyonce. Who doesn't? The girl is fierce. My different likes from some of my black friends has never been a problem, except for once with what I thought was a good friend.

A good friend that I had known since daycare also attended my middle school. We had met each other through our parents and Girl Scouts. Who knew things would change between us. It really was not things that changed, she changed. I remember one day during the first week of middle school I saw her sitting in the cafeteria. She was sitting at a table that had about eight vacant seats. I took my food tray over to her table and got ready to sit down, and to my surprise, she quickly stopped me and said, "All of these seats are saved for my friends." Really? I thought we were friends. I was not embarrassed, but I felt a little shamed and part of me wanted to say, "Excuse the hell out of me!" I went and sat at another table with some more of my friends. I told my mother and she was really surprised. She was more surprised when I told her that the same friend tried to embarrass me in the choir room. My hair was going through changes and was not growing. My MOTHER decided to let her beautician weave a few pieces of hair in the back of my head to make me a thicker ponytail. However, it looked good and nobody knew except my good friends. I recall we were standing getting ready to sing in choir classes. I was on the lower landing and she was two landings above me. Suddenly, I heard, "Look at her with that horse hair! I guess she wants to be all the way white!" It got quiet. I ignored her and prepared to sing. I could not believe she said that in front of so many people. It was not that I was ashamed of my ponytail, but I hate awkward moments that make me stand out. My hair had nothing to do with being white. It had more to do with vanity and my mother's big ideas. After that incident we didn't talk for years, because she changed drastically. She began hanging out with the kids who stayed in trouble. She was suspended a few times and eventually expelled from the school. I think she went to an alternative school for awhile and then who knows where she went. After that my mom kept up with her family and eventually we did talk a little on Facebook, but it was never the same.

This is another reason why it is okay to be different and quirky. Follow your own path. You do not have to walk like others to please them or to make people see you. Stick with those who make you better and who are on the road to success. It will definitely pay off in the long run. Remember, it is only middle school. There is a big wonderful world waiting on quirky you.

People like this particular friend were also the reason I started a mental list in middle school of those I did not like. I like most people unless they have big egos or treat others badly. I hate a bully. I also hated a follower of a certain crowd; a crowd pleaser or a bitch. My criteria went for both boys and girls. Yes, a boy can be a bitch. I don't mean girly bitchy, but boys can think they are better than others and treat them in mean bullying ways. I am a huge believer in treating people the way you want to be treated and if you don't like someone, move on! Leave them alone! If you bully or hate on others, you are dirt! If you watch others being bullied or berated by others, you are worse than the bully. You are a coward! If you can't help the person being bullied, at least tell someone who can. If you are the one being bullied, don't let it happen. You are who you are and way better than the bully. If you walk around with confidence they can't touch you because you don't care. They are like monsters who thrive of people's fears. Don't fear them! Be the quirky warrior and conquer your battles by finding the greatness in you. However, if they are doing something physically demeaning to you, TELL! It is nothing wrong with telling on bullies. You might actually be helping them. Most bullies have problems that are not noticeable, but trust me by high school, well if they make it to high school, you will see that they are nobody! Who do you tell? Tell somebody! We quirky people must stand up for our kind! LOL!

I hate a bully, but I also hate a follower. I never understood why people think they have to be what other people want them to be. If they don't like who you are, they don't deserve your time. There are plenty of people out there who like the things that make you happy. Like me and manga. My friends who liked to read manga as much as I did were a diverse crowd of boys, girls, different races and different grade levels. We did not judge and you know who was invited to the group? EVERYBODY! There are no haters or bullies among manga fans. However, sometimes we can have an ego about manga with those who try to belittle it. What do they know? NOTHING!!!!

Middle school went by fast and I had no major problems. I had my manga friends, I did well in class, I played volleyball, I sang in the choir and I realized what type of people I considered real friends. I also changed my look. No more ugly jeans. It was fitted jeans, black polish and my favorite pair of converse.

Middle school is not easy for a lot of kids because of changing identities. In reality, it is more about the people around you changing than the changes you go through. Recognize the real from the lame, and do what makes you comfortable. It is only middle school. The even bigger deal is coming in high school. So be the boss of you and show them how to do quirky-cool. I did!

Chapter 6 –High School Me

High school is that last step before adulthood. It is all about getting good grades so that you can get into a good college! Wrong! If that were the truth, there would be fewer dropouts, underage drinking, drug users, teen pregnancies and civil disobedience. High school is the place where all the sins of the real world come together and divides all the sins of the world into individual beings. In other words, it produces future ADULTS! All the things we experiment and learn in high school will determine what we do as adults because usually, we either want to exemplify the things we learned or forget them. Either way, it creates a precedent for dealing with future challenges.

Challenges that begin in high school and follow us for the rest of our life include study habits, fashion choices and most of all RELATIONSHIPS! The relationships we form in high school are a precursor to our future relationships. Once again, I thought high school was going to be easy because many of my friends from middle school were attending the same high school. Wrong! Many of my manga friends went to different high schools. My other friends began finding other groups that were more about dating and partying. I had not dated and was not interested. I did like boys and went places in big groups that included boys, but I had not met any boy that I wanted to spend most of my time with or let others see me with. People seeing you with a boyfriend can be a big part of what most high school relationships are about. Nobody wants to look like they are alone or look as if they cannot get a boyfriend. I think from reading manga, talking to my Mom and watching Lifetime movies, I wanted more out of a boyfriend than the silly confused boys I knew in high school. Yes, I said Lifetime movies. For a while, I was hooked on movies about women surviving through different challenges in life. The movies about teen

The Logistics of a Whitewashed Virgin

girls always showed them being dumb over a boy and getting in trouble somehow. At the end, the boy left them, and the girl had to survive on her own. I did not want to be one of those dumb girls. Although, the girls and women in those movies survived and did better in the end, I wanted to be preventive and do better at the beginning.

Lamar High School, where I attended, was probably like most high schools; diverse among the races and the levels of academics. However, in the south there are schools that are predominately black. Some of those schools did well, but it was not what my mother, nor I by this time, was looking for out of an education. Like I said earlier diversity is important to future endeavors and life experiences. Many of the predominately black schools in my area had problems with drugs and gangs. Not that the predominately white schools did not have similar problems, they just hid it well. Additionally, the predominately white schools offered a more rigorous education that, to me, was important in getting into a good university. Moreover, it is more about being able to handle what it takes to stay in the good university rather than just getting in the university. Fortunately, I did so well in middle school that I was able to get into the International Baccalaureate program or I.B. at Lamar.

The Logistics of a Whitewashed Virgin

Although, I encountered all types of people at Lamar, my I.B. classes where predominately white. Most of the blacks were in regular or magnet classes, and unfortunately many of my friends from middle school were also in magnet. An I.B. student can in some ways be a little different in some ways than other students. They are definitely quirky. If you have ever taken any accelerated or honors classes, you know what I mean. It is not only about being smart and figuring out the work. It is also about making good choices, problem solving and most of all, having a smart mouth. Don't tell my Mom, but I admit that I do have a smart mouth. It is something that I.B.

teachers encouraged. They encourage analytical opinions and discussions, and trust me when I say my classes were full of analytical discussions. Some people would call them arguments, but we call them intelligent debates. It was also said that I.B. students had egos. It is not that we had egos, it is that we expect logical conversations and reasoning. All other conversations seem trivial and unnecessary. This way of thinking would be another part of forming my outlook on life. It gave me standards on who I wanted in my immediate circle of friends. I would say family, but my Mother said, I must love my brother and encourage good behavior. He does not make it easy.

The I.B. way of thinking helped me to form standards. Everyone should set standards for their life. There is an old saying that says, "If you do not stand for something, you will fall for anything." I don't know who said it, but I believe it. My standards helped me not fall for peer pressure in high school. In high school, as I said at the beginning of the chapter, we are introduced to a lot of real world challenges that are not good. The two big challenges are drugs and sex. Actually, we are faced with these challenges as early as elementary, but many of us are so young that we believe what our parents, teachers and the children on TV shows tell us. When we get older and develop our own way of thinking, these challenges take on a new twist.

I never had a problem with the challenges of drugs or alcohol because I believed all the stories of how it would ruin my body. I already had enough pressure with trying to stay fit and keep my skin pimple free. All I will say on the body changing issue is, don't let it stress you out. Hormones are natures little tricky way of getting us ready for womanhood. It will get better and remember, if people do not like how you look, they do not deserve your beautiful presence. Shake the lame off and continue on your adventure to greatness.

Since I did not give into peer pressure or trying to be like others, I was not faced with people offering me drugs or alcohol. I did not attend parties where drugs and alcohol was rampant, so no problem. If I did see people drinking or taking drugs, they were definitely not my friends. Remember, I have standards and they did not meet the criteria. I know people like to drink as an adult and I am fine with it as long it is done responsibly, but it is not for me and I am the boss of me. I could get high off or reading manga, although that would soon change.

Drugs are very easy to avoid. Sex and boyfriends are a different story. Sex and boyfriends are almost a traditional requirement to some in high school. It is around you every day in some type of way. Although, I was not attracted to anyone in my high school, I did get offers or should I say suggestions. People were always suggesting who I should date including family members. I remember, I had a good friend that rode the school bus with me. It was a boy and we had known each other since middle school. He was really cool until we got to high school and he needed a date to the homecoming dance. Why did it have to be me? I was enjoying our friendship. We talked on the phone, we had classes together and we hung out sometimes in big groups. Why did he want to confuse our relationship? I never got the impression from him that he liked me for more than a friend. No! I had to hear it from others, including my mother. At my brother's football picnic, he kept coming up to me and my mom making small talk. I did not know why he was acting so nervous. We had known each other for four years, so what was the big deal? "He likes you.", said my mother. She of course, had to inform me at the table with my brother and his friends, who all play on the same team as he does. Everyone looked at me with goofy smiles. I was so embarrassed. It got worse the next day because people kept coming up to me asking me did I like the guy who was my longtime friend. It was horrible! I hate a lot of attention. I like being me, but me does not have to be the center of attention. The gossip and suggestions of us being a couple became so bad that he stopped talking to me. He would not sit with me on the bus and he changed his seat in one of our classes. As you know, I hate drama. I had to put a stop to it.

Eventually, I had a chance to talk with him at the bus stop. I was early and it was only the two of us standing in silence for about ten minutes. Usually, I did not care, but since this was becoming a drama moment for others, I thought talking to him would end this chaos. "What is your problem?" I said in a loud voice. "I may not be talking to you, but I am not deaf," he said this with a smile on his face. We looked at each other and laughed. He explained that because everyone started making a big deal about his interest in me, he tried to back off. He knew how I felt about public attention, so he did not want to push it. Being a silly boy, he thought maybe we should not be friends and the attention would go away. "This is why you are not an I.B. student." I joked. I understood, but unfortunately our relationship was never the same. The uproar over our "getting together" went away and I became known among my friends as the girl with high standards. He eventually started dating a girl in my brother's grade who was what I call a "follower." If that is what he likes, I did not care! Was I jealous? No! Today, he is a junior engineer for a big company. Maybe I should have let go of my standards. Nah! If it is meant to be, it will be.

I kept my standards throughout high school. During the end of high school, I gained a little weight and felt I was not attractive to some guys who liked skinny girls. I did not feel bad about myself, I just knew my limitations. I see girls worrying about certain guys liking them and they become upset and sometimes even suicidal. Really? Over a guy? I don't think so! I might not be his perfect girl, but he is not the only guy in the world. Once again align yourself with people who like and understand the good and bad of you. Perfection does not exist. You exist and everything about you exists and that is what is important. Plus, sometimes we are our own worst critic. It is not as bad as we think.

I did have a conflict with myself on the type of boys I liked. Most of my acquaintances in class were either more quirky than I or they already had girlfriends.

There were some cute boys at Lamar, but they did not like the things I liked and vice versa. I don't settle so no boyfriend for me at that time. I was not worried, but other people would worry like family and some close friends. Either I was always being asked about a boyfriend or someone wanted to fix me up with somebody I did not like. Mostly, I became that girl who listened to everyone's problems. Maybe I should have majored in psychology.

Eventually, one of the biggest events in high school came about. Can you guess? PROM! Prom can be a great thing for some and horrible for others. Although, I did not have a boyfriend, I wanted to go to prom. Luckily for me I had a group of friends that were going together. A few had dates, but mostly everyone was going to hang out. For some girls prom is a big deal. I know girls who dated guys just because they wanted a date to the prom. I did not have a problem going without a date. Sure it is nice to have a date, but it can be fun without a date. I wore a prom dress, got treated like a princess, hung out with my friends, danced and came home late. The only thing I did not do that a lot of girls are pressured to do is have sex. Prom has been known for generations as the time young girls lose their virginity. Of course, there are girls who lost their virginity way before prom, but prom can be a pressure. I can't say when you are ready or who should be ready, but be the boss. Don't do anything to please others. Do what is best for you. Prom can be a big deal, but as usual there is so much more waiting on you out in the world. In reality it is only a dance. Live to dance more than once. Plus, I know people who did not go to prom at all and they ended up just fine. Get past it and get ready for college. You will find your group in college. Plus the boys look better. LOL.

Chapter 7-College Me:

High school was fun. Once again, I did well in my classes, made good friends and I was ready to take on the next part of my journey. I was ready and eager to go to college. Some of my classmates knew what college they wanted to attend since they were little. In Texas, there is always a college battle between University of Texas and Texas A&M. Many of the Lamar High school graduates got into both universities. I did not know what college I wanted to go to, but I knew I wanted a good college that met up to my standards. There were many to choose from, but would they accept me? I was smart, but those types of colleges wanted more than smart. They wanted geniuses with high GPA's and a high score on the SAT. I had a high GPA and I was number 25 in my class ranking, but my SAT score was not high. It did not change my standards, but my standards and their standards were be two different things.

I researched and visited different colleges. I came up with Texas Tech University, University of Texas, Baylor University, and University of Houston. My mother chose Stephen F. Austin in case I could not get into my other choices. I ended up getting accepted to Texas Tech, Baylor University, University of Houston and

Stephen F. Austin. I chose Baylor University. My mom's good friend asked why I did not have any predominately black universities on the list. She and my mother went to Texas Southern University. Remember, I am that so called whitewashed girl. I have never attended a predominately black school except for day care. I know that they are just as good as any university, but I know what I wanted. Plus when it comes to getting certain jobs, employers look at what college you go to and Baylor can stand out among the rest. I had decided to major in accounting and Baylor has a good business school. University of Texas has a good business school, but they did not accept me. Their loss!

Another reason I chose Baylor is because of one of my main standards; making money! All that work I did in grade school has to pay off somehow and I do mean pay. I plan on making good money, so I can have the things I deserve. Remember, I am the boss of me, so the boss should make the big bucks. I know they say college is not for everyone. That may be true, but for me it is the road to riches. Everyone should have goals and a plan on how to achieve those goals. My goals cost. Write down the things you want to do in the future and then plan how you are going to obtain them. If you don't need money, great! Like I said before, my goals cost!

I was so excited about getting into Baylor; however none of my close friends from high school were going there. Most of them were going to University of Houston. There were other students going to Baylor, but they were not close friends. I was alone, but I was okay with it. Since I am quirky cool, I am always looking for new adventures that I can do differently than others. However, leaving home was becoming a bitter sweet moment. I wanted to leave home, but I was used to my spoiled life of having my own room, watching videos on my computer, reading fan fiction and hanging

The Logistics of a Whitewashed Virgin

with my mom. Yes, I said my mom. We became closer the older I got. I started to understand her and she sort of started understanding me. We still differ on who knows whom better. Oh did I forget my little brother? Good! I say "good" because my mom let him use my car when I went away to college and he wrecked it. I did not get another car until my senior year of college. That boy is a problem.

When I first visited Baylor, I noticed there were an abundant amount of white people. I do like diversity, but was I the only black? I know I was not, but I did not see many at first. I know the world has changed, but growing up in the south you hear a lot of stories about being the minority at a predominantly white place. I did not get that feeling at Baylor. It is a religious school and everyone was very nice, but it does help to see somebody from my own race. Of course there are many black students at Baylor and I met many as I continued my stay.

My mom knew I was becoming nervous about going away to college, so she tried to find ways to make me more comfortable. She actually called the school to see if I could be paired up with a black roommate. The lady understood, but could give no guarantees. I hate to admit it, but I was kind of relieved since I did not know anyone going to Baylor. It is not that the race of my roommate mattered so much, but sometimes when you don't know what to expect from a place you never been before, it is comforting to have someone there that may be going through the same types of feelings.

My first time staying at Baylor was in the summer. I attended summer school in June of 2010. I registered late, so I only had one roommate. The dorm room had two rooms with two beds each. My roommate had her own room and I had mine. I know that sounds ideal, but I had no friends at Baylor, so more people would have been nice at the time. Although, I am a friendly person, I am not good at initiating friendships. My roommate seemed nice, but we were totally different. I like to be in my room reading fan fiction or watching videos on the computer. She was a jogger and apparently had a few friends that went to Baylor. She tried to connect with me, but I was so into what I was used to doing that we did not connect. It is sad that I don't remember her name. I feel bad about it today. Actually, I missed out on a lot of activities that summer for new students. Because I registered late, I did not get the notices about the freshman orientation. People were meeting and having fun while I was on my computer hoping the summer would pass quickly. I ended up passing both my classes that summer. It ended and that was it. I have nothing exciting to tell about my summer at Baylor before my freshman year. Yes, it was my fault, but I guess I was not ready.

I enjoyed the rest of my summer at home, but it ended fast. I knew I had to go away, but school did not motivate me about my college life. I told myself that it would be better in the fall semester because there would be more people and definitely more freshman. I would make friends and it would be a great college life.

On my first day of fall semester at Baylor, my mother and brother drove me to the dorm. Baylor is good at having volunteer students help you unload your stuff and carry it to the room. I was excited and nervous. There were so many people. I was ready to meet my roommate. Remember, I said my mom had called to see if she could get me a black roommate? Well that did not happen. She was white. I did not care, but she looked a little old. She was my age, but she looked old. I had a feeling this might not work out, but I am always open to new things. My mom who is a big talker started talking to her and her mom and found out many interesting things. We did not talk much and she did not seem that interested. I think we both expected different roommates.

The Logistics of a Whitewashed Virgin

After my mom's conversation, all I knew was that my roommate's name was Sydney. Apparently, she did not want to go to Baylor, but her boyfriend went to a college near Baylor. Oh great, I thought. This is not starting off good. I met her boyfriend a few times and he was nice, but I think he could tell this was not an ideal roommate arrangement. At least, she did not have him sleep over or take up the room with college sexual needs. Unfortunately, a lot of people I knew had problems with their roommates boyfriends always being in the room. Sydney was mostly gone to class, working or with her boyfriend. Thank goodness!

The Logistics of a Whitewashed Virgin

After we got through decorating my side of the room and putting up all my stuff, it was time for my mom and brother to leave. I wished they could have stayed, but I knew they had to go. It is amazing how no matter how old I get, sometimes I enjoy being my mother's little girl. I am not a big *huggy* type of person, but I did like it when my mom hugged me. I did not show it, but I missed her already. Bye mommy! So now it was just me and my roommate Sydney.

Sydney and I did not talk much, but it was okay because there were so many freshman things to do all week. Baylor is good at making freshman feel comfortable. The freshman had so many activities that included big groups and small groups. Moreover, my roommate and I had to meet with the dorm hall leader about how to get along as roommates. I really hoped that we could get along. Unfortunately, we did not. We were roommates for one year and we barely talked. When we argued, we did not talk. Instead, we made annoying noises, well at least she did. She would slam things like books or make noises eating. I began hating the sound of fish shaped crackers and the smell of peanut butter. Thank goodness for headphones. I did not make noises, but I was always in the room. I think she hated me always being there. Sometimes, I would talk loud when my mom called on purpose.

It was weird, but it was us. Unless you already know your roommate, you never know who you might get. Sydney was not as bad as some other roommates I heard about. We did eventually have a great conversation at the end of the year. It was during a hurricane drill. We sat beside each other in the hallway, and she was very talkative. It was the end of school and Sydney was happy about leaving Baylor for another college. It was the first time I saw her funny and friendly side. Too bad it came at the end.

Whatever college you attend, make sure you try to work with your roommate on what you like and don't like. You also have to respect their likes and dislikes. It can be a great experience or one of the worst in your life. Whatever your situation, it will help you realize the kind of person you are and the type of people you can tolerate. It is amazing that as I got older, I realized I can be picky about who I let into my space. I see it as a good thing. Remember, it is all about STANDARDS!

My freshman year went by quickly. Sydney and I never had any type of friendship. We did not talk. She did not like Baylor and she did not return after freshman year was over. I made a few friends and I passed my classes. Baylor is one of those universities that I call "In a

The Logistics of a Whitewashed Virgin

bubble." What I mean by "In a bubble" is that it's a place isolated from the "goings on" of the world around it. In this case, the world around it is the city of Waco, Texas. Baylor University is a university that is in the small town of Waco. Waco is one of those sleepy little country towns that has a history of cattle drives and a religious cult that was destroyed by federal forces. Most of my experiences in college were on the campus. Many students that came in the year I did began staying off campus by their junior year. Not me! I stayed and enjoyed it.

One reason I enjoyed Baylor is because of the organizations that I joined. It is important to join some sort of club or organization. At college you can find something that fits who you are. If you are not a group type of person, you can find other people who are the same as you, but they are a group. Does that make sense? Doesn't matter, it is college.

I knew I did not want to be in a Greek organization because I am that person who does not feel that I need a group to make me into who I want to be. I don't have anything against Greek organizations; it is just that they are not for me. However, some people feel that since I am black, it is required that I either join the black Greeks or no Greeks. There are other groups, but they all seem to be predominately one race. However there are a few multi-cultural Greek groups, but again I am not the Greek type. I don't party enough, date enough or drink enough. I know that Greek organizations do so much more with community service and outreach, especially as the members get older and graduate college. I recommend you check into them and find the group that fits you. They can have a different atmosphere on every campus.

I don't do anything the same way as one group. It would mess up my quirky-cool, but somehow I ended up in a Greek organization that was coed. I was looking for a group that would look good on my resume as an accountant. I was already in different honor roll groups and I joined a business women's group, but I needed something known in the business world, so I signed up for a business Greek organization. Foolish me. I though all I had to do was sign up and I was in. Wrong! We actually had to pledge and do crazy activities. The organization is well known in the business world, and I knew it would look good on my resume. The college part of the organization is similar to other Greek organizations. The only difference is we don't do step shows. I knew people who pledged and it took up a lot of their time. I said that would never be me and there I was during the spring semester of my second year dressing funny, staying up late and wishing for sleep. One thing about college is, you will sometimes do things outside of your comfort zone. I was definitely outside of my comfort zone, but I completed my tasks and became part of this well-known business organization.

My organization is great for business majors; however, it does have a reputation of being snobby and being a predominately white group. On some campuses, it has a reputation of not recruiting blacks. My chapter did recruit blacks, but not many made it pass the interview process. I don't know what they were looking for, but they chose me. When I pledged there were two black girls already in the group and one other black girl who pledged along with me. In fact my "Big" was a black girl. A "Big" is like a big sister or brother in the Greek organization. It is like a mentor.

At first, it did not matter to me. I was only in the group for what it would do for my future career endeavors. Eventually, my perspective and politics about the group would change. I did not do everything the group did, and I made it clear that I don't party. I know people think of college as being the time to party hard, but I was different. I do like going places, but partying where there is drinking and other activities, is not what I like to do. I like being in control of what I do and to me drinking takes over that control. If you choose to drink, don't do it because of other people. I have seen a lot of people get in trouble in college because of drinking. It is not worth it. I did go to a few simple parties that were more about hanging out than drinking, but it was only a few. Most of my outside activities in college included campus events, a few campus concerts, a few football games, and outings with friends. I did do all of the other activities in my Greek organization like community service and meetings. I tried to get into recruiting by inviting some of my black friends to join, but they never passed the interview process. I began to think like others about the group that they did not want blacks and other minorities or at least they wanted a certain type. I saw some great minority candidates come through, but none made it through. I stopped recruiting because I was frustrated with the group, and I did not want to put anyone through the process for nothing. I probably could have spoken up more, but that would have been a bigger battle than I could handle at the time. I did start to understand why some people did not join my Greek organization, and the sentiments of some black students. Overall, the organization did keep me busy with community service and meetings. I enjoyed helping people in the community. The group did what I first intended it to do, but I wished more minorities could have been a part of the process. Maybe it is different on other college campuses.

Being in college classes is similar across every university when it comes to your major. It is fun when you start taking the classes, but there are always those classes that are so difficult that you wonder why you chose that major. Luckily, there are ways to check on the teaching styles of the professors, but there is always that one class that has that one anal professor. No matter how hard you try to get around taking that class, there are no other choices. Luckily, the rigor of my high school classes and the International Baccalaureate program helped me prepare for such classes. Well some of them. Don't be afraid to take challenging classes in high school. It helps! The only thing the rigorous classed did not help me with was speaking in front of a crowd. I hate it! Hate is a strong word, but it is so appropriate for me when it comes to public speaking.

I don't mind talking to people and I don't mind group presentations, but when it comes to me speaking alone, I can't do it. My knees get shaky and I feel like I am going to faint. One of the first classes most people take in college is speech. If you think your major will not require speech, you are probably WRONG! Get ready because it is not as easy as reading off of some index cards for a minute and sit down. No! There are essays and critiques. It is horrible. My mother continues to say that I will get over it as I get older. I don't feel that way. It has not happened yet, and I don't believe it will ever happen. With all the new technology today, my generation does not need to talk in front of a group. Give me a power point presentation any day.

The times that I had to get up in front of the entire class were horrible. Not only was I nervous, but I worried about everything. I could not focus on the speech. I worried about how I looked, how I spoke and what people were thinking. I had no strategy. I read the strategies. I wrote them down, but when I got up to speak, it all went out the window. I think the worst part was when the professor tried to give me advice. She happened to be a black teacher. The only black teacher I had my entire time at Baylor. "You need to breathe before you get up to speak and the more you practice, the better you will do on your speech," she said as she tried to console me after one of my panic attacks. It did not help. Then she played the civil rights card, by saying, "There are not many black girls at Baylor who are here strictly because of academics. You are a role model and you need to present yourself in such a way that will inspire other black girls." What? Was she talking to the quirky, whitewashed, sheltered, computer girl? One thing I have never had to do is stand up for any racial issues. I did know about the historical struggles and achievements of black people, but "fighting the power" were not my motto. Don't get me wrong, I do have opinions, and I keep up with some political issues. I voted for Obama, but the most I did at a predominately conservative school, is wearing an Obama tee shirt when he won. I got a few looks and that was it. That is my struggle and my fight. That is as far as it goes. If I have inspired anyone, it was not by choice. Well unless you count this book. Lol. Somehow, I got through that treacherous speech class and all my other classes. Did I ever fail a class? Yes, I admit it. One of my problems is procrastination. I do like to wait until the last minute. However, I usually get the job done. College is totally different. In high school you can wait until the last minute and do the work overnight or ask the teacher for more time for some lame reason. Not in college. On some assignments, if you wait too long there is never enough time. You realize at the last minute how much work it takes to complete, so you don't complete it. The best thing is to write things down or post it. I love post its. I know it sounds naggy, but it will help in the long run when you are trying to graduate and get your GPA up to something that you can list on a job application. I still procrastinate, and I usually suffer through it. However, I don't recommend it.

Okay are you ready to hear about my boyfriend? Good, so am I. No, I do not and did not have a boyfriend during college. I had offers and I have friends, but a fall in love, have sex in the dorm and skip classes because I want to be with my man boyfriend, did not happen for me. This is one reason I could focus on getting through college in three years, plus I saw so many girls fall behind or drop out of college because they were worried more about their boyfriend than about getting through college. I think it is good to have a boyfriend in college as long as he is moving in the same direction as you. He should not hold you back from your goals. He should help you get there and he should have his own goals. If you find yourself thinking about him more than you are thinking about yourself, you are not going in the right direction. It is college. It is okay to be selfish when it comes to what you want. It should be all about you! YOLO! There is plenty of time to give to a husband, kids and jobs. For me it is about travel and money. I want to make money and I want to travel. Now if I can find a boyfriend who wants to do the same things and he is quirky-cool, then that will work.

Being the quirky-cool girl can cause problems with me having a boyfriend. They must like the things I like. During high school and after my manga and anime phase, I got into my biggest obsession; KPOP! If you do not know KPOP, you must be old as my grandparents. KPOP is South Korean pop music and I love it. In fact, I love everything about South Korea. I love it so much that I took a Korean language class. Yes, I speak a little Korean, but in order to be fluent in it, I need to immerse myself in the culture. Therefore, one of my main goals after college is to visit Korea. Everyone I know, including my mother, knows my obsession and is familiar with KPOP. They have no choice. This is why any boyfriend I have would need to be able to handle my obsession. He would need to get ready to pack his bag and travel into my quirky world. My mom said I must want a Korean boyfriend because she does not know any black boys that like KPOP. I do. Although, I don't know many black KPOP boys, but I know they are out there. It is not necessarily about the race for me. It is more about who they are and do they fit with me and my ambitions. My mom says I am picky. I say I just have standards. We all should set standards for what we want in life. Will they change as we get older? Yes, but setting standards is the key to getting what you need. It may take longer than you want, but be patient. It is better than settling for garbage. Trust me. I have seen some girls who are stuck with garbage and it smells bad.

The rest of my college life went well. Sure if I could go back, I would make some changes, but I did not have a guide book like this one to help me; lucky you. I made some great friends and I even met a few KPOP obsessed people. Yes, we are everywhere and we are taking over. College is about academics and a social life. It is the beginning of adulthood, so go and find who you are going to be. If things don't seem that great right now, wait. I promise it gets better.

Keep being you and be in control of you. Don't let other people's expectations dominate who you are. Have standards and enjoy the things you like. If the people around you do not understand you, that is their loss. Maybe you don't understand them either. Nonetheless, what you do and who you are is important to this world, and the world could not rotate without us quirky-cool beings.

Chapter 8-Future Me

I graduated! I have the whole world in front of me. I am ready and excited about my future. I think I am prepared for the challenges that the world has in store for me. All of my quirky-cool adventures from elementary through college have shaped and guided me down a sometime bumpy path, but also a contiguous path of culture, imagination and determination.

The first thing I will do is GET A JOB! I am ready to work and see where my accounting and international business degrees lead me. I don't think I will stay in accounting forever because there are so many opportunities that I am searching for along my path. I do know I want to work in international business for a nonprofit company. I want to help people and travel while making money. Remember, money is important for my standards because the second thing that I will definitely do is travel to South Korea. I need to immerse myself into the language and culture and meet some KPOP stars. Daebok!

    I guess we will see what will happen. When will I go to South Korea? Will I get a good paying job? Will I find my true love? Will he be able to put up with quirky-cool me? The answers to all of these questions are yet to be seen! Until then stay QUIRKY-COOL!!!!

www.ingramcontent.com/pod-product-compliance
Lightning Source LLC
Chambersburg PA
CBHW071230090426
42736CB00014B/3023